T0057414

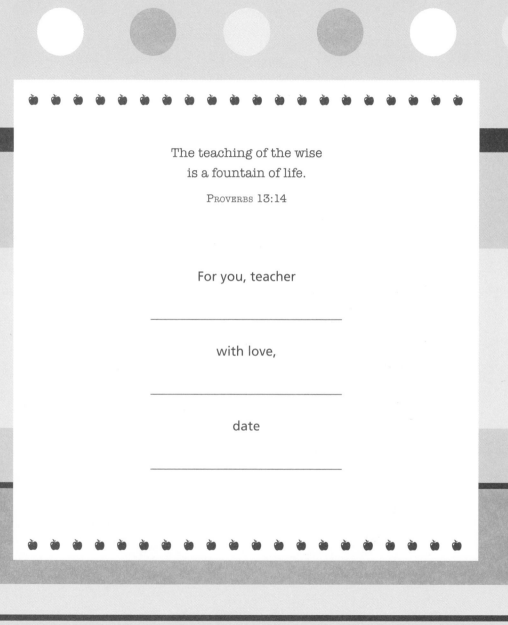

The teaching of the wise
is a fountain of life.

PROVERBS 13:14

For you, teacher

_____

with love,

_____

date

_____

It is a greater work to educate a child
than to rule a state.

WILLIAM ELLERY CHANNING

The **BEST** TEACHER in the **WORLD**

HOWARD BOOKS
A DIVISION OF SIMON & SCHUSTER
New York   London   Toronto   Sydney

Our purpose at Howard Books is to:

- *Increase faith* in the hearts of growing Christians
- *Inspire holiness* in the lives of believers
- *Instill·hope* in the hearts of struggling people everywhere

Because He's coming again!

Published by Howard Books, a division of Simon & Schuster, Inc.
1230 Avenue of the Americas, New York, NY 10020
www.howardpublishing.com

HOWARD BOOKS

The Best Teacher in the World © 2007 by Dave Bordon & Associates, LLC

Library of Congress Cataloging-in-Publication Data

The best teacher in the world / [edited by Chrys Howard].
   p. cm.
 Includes bibliographical references.
 ISBN-13: 978-1-4165-4209-4
 ISBN-10: 1-4165-4209-4
 ISBN-13: 978-1-58229-696-8 (gift ed.)
 ISBN-10: 1-58229-696-0 (gift ed.)
 1. Teaching—Religious aspects—Christianity. 2. Teachers—Religious life. I. Howard, Chrys, 1953–
 BV4596.T43B47 2007
 242'.68—dc22

         2007015585

10 9 8 7 6 5 4 3 2 1

HOWARD and colophon are registered trademarks of Simon & Schuster, Inc.

Manufactured in the United States of America

For information regarding special discounts for bulk purchases, please contact: Simon & Schuster Special Sales at 1-800-456-6798 or business@simonandschuster.com.

Project developed by Bordon Books, Tulsa, Oklahoma
Project writing and compilation by Shawna McMurry and Christy Phillippe in association with Bordon Books
Edited by Chrys Howard
Cover design by Lori Jackson, LJ Design

CONTENTS

Introduction 7

YOU'RE THE BEST TEACHER IN THE WORLD BECAUSE . . .

You Encourage Me When I Need It 9

You Help Me See Things from a New Perspective 21

You Make Learning Fun 35

You Are Patient and Understanding 47

You Care About Me 61

You Take the Time to Listen 75

You Are a Good Influence in My Life 87

You Bring Out the Best in Me 99

You Inspire Me to Achieve My Dreams 113

Notes 128

One hundred years from now,

it will not matter what my bank account was,

the sort of house I lived in,

or the kind of car I drove . . .

but the world may be different because

I was important in the life of a child.

FOREST E. WITCRAFT

INTRODUCTION

Teachers who stand out among their peers are the ones who genuinely care about the well-being of their students. They are also kind, patient, understanding, fun-loving, and inspiring. A tall order for anyone, surely—yet you're holding this book because someone recognized these qualities in you and thinks you are quite simply the best teacher in the world.

Whether you are just beginning your journey as a teacher or have been molding young minds for many years, be encouraged and refreshed by the touching stories, personal prayers, devotional reflections, and inspirational quotes and poems chosen just for you. And as you read, may you be reminded of how very much you are loved and appreciated.

You're the

BEST

TEACHER

in the World Because…

You Encourage Me
When I Need It.

A professor can

never better

distinguish himself

in his work

than by encouraging

a clever pupil,

for the true

discoverers are

among them,

as comets amongst

the stars.

CAROLUS LINNAEUS

Correction does much, but encouragement does more.

JOHANN WOLFGANG VON GOETHE

An important part of your life calling as a teacher is to be a source of encouragement for your students, and it's a job you take very seriously and perform with excellence. But who is there to encourage you when you're feeling run down or discouraged?

God is always there to lend a listening ear, and He's provided countless words of encouragement just for you in the Scriptures.

He also instructs us to seek refuge in other believers and to be a source of encouragement for each other. Is there another teacher at your school who is a believer and who would be willing to become your prayer partner? Or maybe there are many believers at your school who would be blessed by the strength and encouragement a prayer group provides.

Take time to be refreshed and encouraged yourself so you'll be ready when your students need your encouragement.

A LETTER TO MY TEACHER

Dear Teacher,

You are always there with a word of encouragement when I need it the most. You seem to know just what to say to make me feel valuable and capable of the task that lies ahead. Your loving words inspire me to reach for greatness and give me hope, even when the circumstances around me seem dismal.

Thank you for the loving encouragement that you so freely give. I hope you know how valuable your contribution is in my life and in the lives of all your students. Thank you for your sensitivity to the needs of my heart.

Sincerely,

Your Student

A pat on the back

is only a

few vertebrae

removed from

a kick in the pants,

but is miles ahead

in results.

ELLA WHEELER WILCOX

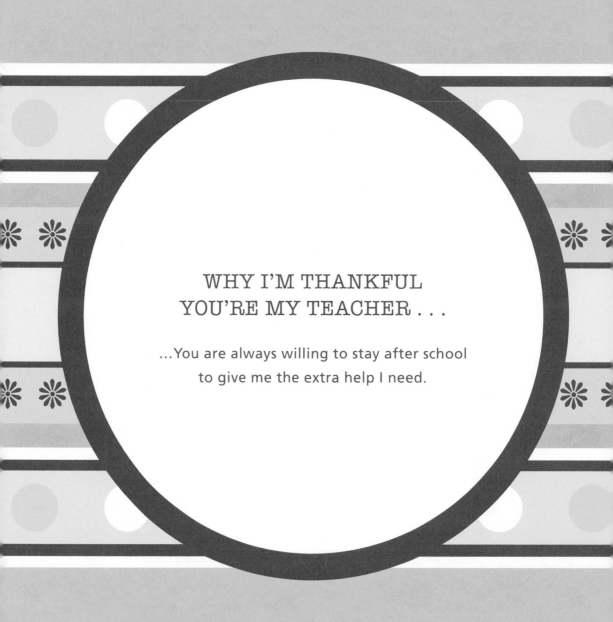

WHY I'M THANKFUL
YOU'RE MY TEACHER . . .

. . . You are always willing to stay after school
to give me the extra help I need.

ONE DROP IN THE POND

BY CARRIE YOUNCE

Unlike some in his profession, my sixth-grade English teacher—Mr. Duncan—seemed to realize that the true blessing of being a teacher is in the opportunity to help shape a human soul.

Since I attended nine schools in twelve years, it seemed as if I was always the "new kid." After turning in one particularly lengthy poetry assignment, Mr. Duncan asked me to stay after class.

"This is very good," he said. "And very sad. Why are you so sad?"

When I complained that I just didn't fit in, Mr. Duncan folded his hands on his desk and said, "Look at my fingers. They all have a place. They all fit. That's the way God made it. You also have a place. The adventure is in finding it."

"Is the poem really good?" I asked. "I mean, I want to be really good like Stephen King or Shakespeare."

"Why do you want to be like someone else? You are capable of so much more than that. Just be yourself; be spectacular."

He encouraged me to push toward the edge. "There are no boundaries set for excellence," he proclaimed. "There are only guidelines that, if followed, will yield much good fruit." In this, he taught me that I could do whatever I wanted to do—that the power to become whatever I was called to be already lay within me.

I was fertile ground for the seeds of acceptance that he planted in me.

Mr. Duncan not only believed in me, but he also constantly affirmed that the Greater One in me was doing the work through me.

"All good things come from God. You're the receiver of a gift. Don't try to take too much credit."

I developed appreciation for the grace of God within that simple truth.

When Mr. Duncan passed away three years after I left his class, more than four hundred people attended his funeral. Past students and their parents, fellow teachers, and neighbors all came to mourn and pay respect to the man whom we called teacher, mentor, and friend.

One of the poems read by the pastor at his memorial was mine. It was a simple free verse, speaking of how a drop of water falling onto the surface of a pond makes many ripples. The pastor closed by saying, "This one man has affected the lives of everyone here. Like in this poem, he was one drop that fell to earth and landed here in this pond, right where he belonged. He rose up here and took his proper place, so that we all might grow."

My poem, the one he had called good but sad, was added to the testimony of his legacy. I guess, in the end, God made teachers of us both.[1]

> Those who are lifting the world upward and onward
> are those who encourage more than criticize.
>
> ELIZABETH HARRISON

Heavenly Father,

Thank You for being there with a word of assurance and encouragement when I need it most. There are moments when I can see the effects of my efforts, see the lights coming on in the minds of my students. Maybe a student will come to my desk with the sparkle of confidence in his eyes, thanking me for staying after school to explain a concept he was having difficulty with. He proudly exclaims, "I get it, now."

Then there are days when I feel so ineffective in my classroom—as if nothing I do is producing any change in my students' lives. It's easy to get discouraged. But when I meet with You in prayer and read your Word, You never fail to provide the confidence and motivation I need to keep working, guiding my students toward a bright future.

Just as You encourage me when my confidence is ebbing, help me to be a source of strength for my students when they are feeling down. Give me the wisdom to know how to prod them toward excellence in their studies without dampening their spirits. Most of all, give me opportunities to guide them toward You, the ultimate Source of strength and encouragement.

Amen.

I THANK GOD for you,

my ENCOURAGING teacher!

You're the

BEST

TEACHER

in the World Because…

You Help Me See

Things from a New

Perspective.

Many ideas grow better when
transplanted into another mind than in
the one where they sprung up.

OLIVER WENDELL HOLMES

Do not conform any longer to the pattern of this world,
but be transformed by the renewing of your mind.
Then you will be able to test and approve what God's will
is—his good, pleasing and perfect will.

ROMANS 12:2

We all experience burnout from time to time. Even the best teachers will sometimes wonder if their efforts are really making a difference.

When you're feeling discouraged, maybe it's time to renew your mind, to view your situation from a different perspective. Take a few minutes to reflect on an encouraging scripture. Seize the opportunity during your lunch break to go outside, get a breath of fresh air, and notice the beauty of God's creation. Or perhaps a weekend getaway is in order.

Removing yourself from the source of your discouragement, even for a few minutes, will help you to clear your mind. You'll be able to see God more clearly and also see His plan being worked out in your life.

A TEACHER'S TRIBUTE TO HER STUDENTS

For the last twenty-two years, I have been a paraeducator for the mentally handicapped. These particular citizens have accomplished what most of us long for. These children can teach like no one else the supremacy of love over gifts. They will never be brain surgeons, but they have taught me and many others the value of long-suffering, forgiveness, endurance, compassion, humility, and purity of thought.

These kids have it mastered when it comes to love. I often think of them as being the ones who have accomplished the true understanding of 1 Corinthians 13. They are patient and kind. They aren't proud, boastful, envious, rude, or self-seeking. They are slow to become angry and quick to forget an offense. They rejoice in the good and shun evil. They protect, trust, hope, and persevere. They are the true teachers.

Thank You, Lord, for granting me the privilege of serving these students.

SHARON RICKARD

The mind of a child

is fascinating,

for it looks on old things

with new eyes.

F. Scott Fitzgerald

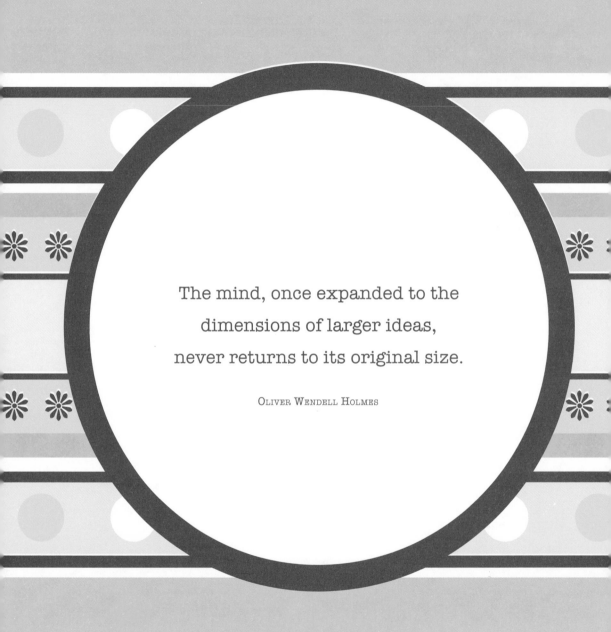

The mind, once expanded to the dimensions of larger ideas, never returns to its original size.

THE SUNDAY SCHOOL TEACHER

By Robin Lee Shope

When the pastor escorted the new Sunday school teacher, Miss Betty Ray, in to meet her pseudo-angelic-looking class, she didn't know what she was in for. New in town, she hadn't heard of their reputation for chasing off teachers. By the look of her pink dress, one size too small, and her bad blonde bleach job, the students felt they had an easy mark. Soon bets were being taken as to how long Miss Betty would last with them.

Betty introduced herself, stating she recently came from the South. Snickers rippled in the room as she rummaged through the huge shoulder bag she carried for a purse.

"Have any of you ever been out of state?" she asked in a friendly tone. A few hands went up.

"Anyone visit *outside* the country?"

No hands went up now. The silent teens were puzzled. What did this have to do with anything? Finally, Betty's hand struck on what she had been searching for in her handbag. Pulling out a long tube, she unrolled a map of the world.

"What else do you have in there? Lunch?" someone cracked. Betty smiled lightly and answered, "Cookies." Then she pointed with a long fingernail to an odd-shaped continent.

Everyone craned their neck to see where it was.

"Is that Texas?" someone sitting in the back asked.

"Not even close. It's India." Her eyes twinkled with joy. "My parents were missionaries there, and that is where my mother was when I came into the world." Betty fumbled again with her purse, this time pulling out a handful of wrinkled pictures along with a tin of chocolate-chip cookies. They passed the pictures around, viewing each with great interest. Dark faces stared up from the photos, frozen in time.

"You don't have to be a missionary—everyone can do something in this world to help another," Miss Betty said. The hour quickly slid by as she told them her stories about faraway places and what the people were like there.

Sunday after Sunday, Betty went to class, tying her lessons to their everyday lives. She told the teens how they could make a difference right now. The students grew to love her, bleached blonde hair and all.

Betty taught that Sunday school class for twenty years. Although she never married or had children of her own, the town came to think of her as a surrogate parent.

At last, her hair grew into a natural gray. Increasing wrinkles about her mouth and eyes added character to her cherubic face. Her hands began to shake with age. Every now and then, she received a letter from a former student. There was a doctor, a research scientist, a home-maker, a businessman, and many teachers among them.

One day she reached into her mailbox and pulled out a blue envelope with a familiar foreign stamp in the upper-right-hand corner. In the left corner was the name of a boy in that very first Sunday school class, years ago. She recalled how he'd always liked her cookies and seemed so interested in her lessons. A picture slid out of the envelope and onto her lap. Squinting her eyes, she smiled at the man in the photo, still seeing the teenage boy in him. Standing in rubble, in the city of Delhi, India, he stood with other volunteers who had come to help earthquake victims.

The caption read: "Because of you, I am here now."[2]

By instilling in your student
a passion for learning
and an inquisitive mind,
you are planting the seeds
of a changed life.

D. Valentine

I'll always remember my junior high music teacher, Dr. Dietmann, because he touched my life in many different ways. He encouraged me when I needed it and gave me extra time in order to help me keep up with my classmates. But not only that, he opened up the world of music for me, causing me to appreciate all different genres and styles. He'll probably never know what he meant to me, but whenever I listen to classical music, I think of him and realize what a difference he made in my life.

LACEE BROWN

The object of teaching a child is to enable him
to get along without a teacher.

ELBERT HUBBARD

Heavenly Father,

I think it's so important for my students to be able to see the world through another's point of view. Not only does looking at something from a different perspective help them to gain more knowledge on the subject; it also helps them to be more understanding of others, to be able to relate with people from all different walks of life.

I rely on You for the inspiration I need to create an open-minded environment in my classroom. Give me new and creative ideas about how to get my students to dig for the answers, approaching each question from several different angles to gain a fuller understanding of the world around them.

I also ask that You daily provide me with a fresh perspective about my work, my students, even my relationship with You. Help me to never grow stagnant in my ideas but to continue to learn and grow. In this way, I'll be able to serve as an example to my students.

Thank You, Lord, for renewing my mind.

Amen.

I THANK GOD for you,

my THOUGHT-PROVOKING teacher!

You're the

BEST

TEACHER

in the World Because...

You Make

Learning Fun.

What we learn with pleasure

we never forget.

ALFRED MERCIER

Let them praise his name with dancing
and make music to him with tambourine and harp.
For the LORD takes delight in his people.

PSALM 149:3-4

Just as you take joy in seeing your students having fun while they are learning, God delights in seeing you have fun as you learn and grow in your relationship with Him.

If your devotional life has grown a bit dull, spice things up a bit. Sing a favorite hymn to God or attend a praise concert. Take a hike and let the beauty of creation penetrate your soul. Sketch or paint a picture that expresses your feelings about God. Listen to a favorite Christian music CD. You may even feel compelled to dance before your Maker. Or maybe you enjoy playing an instrument or would have fun learning to play a new one and using it to convey your thoughts toward God.

He delights in your communication with Him, no matter what form it takes, and He loves to see you having fun in the many avenues of expression He's provided for you to enjoy.

A LETTER TO MY TEACHER

Dear Teacher,

I look forward to school each day because you make learning so much fun. There is never a dull moment in our classroom. Whether you're telling a joke or doing an experiment or having us participate in some unusual project, you have this contagious energy that makes me want to laugh and smile and become a part of things. There's no sitting in the back row passing notes in your class because no one wants to miss out on the fun. I can tell you're really having a great time teaching us, too, and that makes me feel loved and accepted. I'm learning all kinds of things I didn't know before, and it doesn't even feel like I'm trying.

Thank you for being such a fun and energetic teacher. It's obvious that you have passion for what you're doing. Please keep the creative ideas coming.

Sincerely,

Your Student

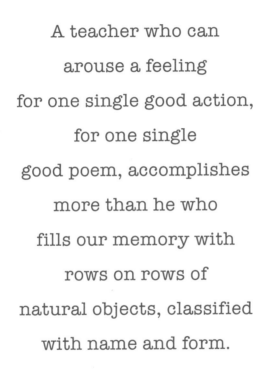

A teacher who can
arouse a feeling
for one single good action,
for one single
good poem, accomplishes
more than he who
fills our memory with
rows on rows of
natural objects, classified
with name and form.

JOHANN WOLFGANG VON GOETHE

Nothing great was ever achieved
without enthusiasm.

RALPH WALDO EMERSON

TEACHING MISS PICKLE

By Shae A. Cooke

"You can always tell Miss Pickle by her crunch!" giggled Rebecca.

"Sssshhh, she's coming down the hall. We had better get to class," I warned.

Miss Pickle was our school principal—she also taught third grade and happened to be my teacher. She was a woman of a certain age—ninety, one hundred, one hundred fifty? It didn't matter to a child of eight, going on eight and a half. Old is old—period; though I am sure that when she was a child there was no such thing as "history class."

Her straight gray hair had a slight blue tint to it, and she wore it in a bun high atop her head. And she was short—so short, in fact, that she could have posed on top of my soccer trophy. Her onion-like skin was dry and transparent, and her wrinkles deep and furrowed. She looked a lot like Granny on *The Beverly Hillbillies* television show—old-fashioned and stern. She was the sort of teacher we sat up straight for, even when she just passed by in our thoughts.

"Good morning, class," she cackled. Becky and I took our seats. "Pull out your English assignments for today."

"I forgot to do it!" I whispered to my friend. A dark cloud rolled across the blank page, where definitions were supposed to be. I looked up and there she stood—hands on bony hips and a disappointed frown.

"I . . . I thought it was due next week, Miss Pickle."

"Miss Manuel," she replied. "You must *yearn* to learn—you'll stay after school to complete it."

My hazel eyes rolled skyward. "Um . . . yes, ma'am," I replied.

After she dismissed the class, I remained at my desk and pulled out my workbook—this was going to be tough. Miss Pickle drew up a chair beside me. "Remember what I said earlier?" she asked. I nodded. "What can I do to motivate you to learn and to have your assignments in on time?" My jaw dropped.

She's asking me? I thought. Okay, I'd take the bait.

"Well . . . for one, you could make learning more fun!" There, I had said it, and I readied myself to bolt. After all, she'd been teaching for a hundred years, so who was I to tell her what to do?

"I see," she said, rubbing her chin whiskers and nodding like a bobble-head doll. "Tell you what. You run along home now and finish your assignment there. I'll see you in class tomorrow—and thank you for your honesty." Whoa! I walked out of the classroom dazed—this was a close encounter of the strangest kind.

The school bell rang the following morning, and we took our seats and pulled out our spelling worksheets. Miss Pickle hadn't arrived yet, so I recited the events of the afternoon before with Rebecca. Our conversation came to an abrupt end, however, as music blared over our class intercom.

"Wha . . .?" The classroom door opened—and in came Miss Pickle dressed as a . . . well, a pickle . . . with an oversized encyclopedia in her hand. She faced the class, cleared her throat, and belted out a rendition of "The Encyclopedia Song," as sung by Jiminy Cricket on *The Mickey Mouse Club.*

"Encyclopedia," she sang. "E-N-C-Y-C-L-O-P-E-D-I-A. You just look inside this book and you will see—every letter here from 'A' to 'Z.' Encyclopedia. E-N-C-Y-C-L-O-P-E-D-I-A!"

Thirty-one jaws dropped. Then suddenly, as she sang the last long, drawn-out, cackly "A," everyone burst out laughing and applauded her wildly.

She winked and smiled at me. From that day on, Miss Pickle had my complete devotion and attention in the hallways and classroom. I loved the courage it took for her to stand in front of a class, at one hundred fifty-something years old, and sing—especially in the pickle outfit. I loved the fact that she cared about us enough to go to such lengths to ensure we enjoyed learning, and I became eager to perform well. If she went that far, I certainly didn't want to let her down by not doing my very best![3]

Above all things we must take care that the child,
who is not yet old enough to love his studies,
does not come to hate them and dread the bitterness
which he once tasted, even when the years of infancy are left behind.
His studies must be made an amusement.

QUINTILIAN

🍎 🍎 🍎 🍎 🍎

Precious Lord,

I love to see my students having fun while they are learning. It's one of a teacher's greatest joys to see students genuinely enjoying the activities planned for them and broadening their minds in the process.

Please continue to provide me with creative ideas to make the lessons I teach fun for my students. Thank You for the many resources that are available now. Guide me to those that will be most helpful and most appropriate for my students. Help me to learn my students' personalities —their likes and dislikes—as well as their learning styles, so I'll know which activities will suit them best.

Renew my energy so I'll be a fun and energetic presence in my classroom. When I'm having fun teaching, my students are much more likely to have fun learning. Thank You for Your abiding joy that You've blessed me with and for the students who make that joy bubble over.

Amen.

I THANK GOD for you,

my FUN and CREATIVE teacher!

You're the

BEST

TEACHER

in the World Because...

You Are Patient and
Understanding.

The fruit of the Spirit is . . .

patience.

GALATIANS 5:22

As God's chosen people, holy and dearly loved,
clothe yourselves with compassion,
kindness, humility, gentleness and patience.

COLOSSIANS 3:12

Patience is one of the most important attributes you can bring into your classroom. It's a rare quality in today's world and something your students may not experience elsewhere. Your ability to exhibit patience in your dealings with your students will not be unnoticed or go unrewarded.

Students who are taught in an atmosphere governed by patience and understanding will likely feel more freedom to participate in class. They'll also be less likely to give up on themselves if they're unable to grasp a concept right away. And they'll tend to follow your example, extending patience to you and to their classmates.

If you're struggling to maintain patience, remember the incredible patience God extends toward us and the amazing love from which His patience flows. By extending this patience to your students, you're demonstrating to them in concrete, understandable terms the wonder of God's love.

A LETTER TO MY TEACHER

Dear Teacher,

I feel so blessed to have a teacher who is patient and understanding. When I'm struggling with my work, you never scold me or embarrass me in front of the class because I don't understand something. Instead, you've many times stayed after school to work with me until I'm able to grasp a new concept. You never get irritated with me, at least not outwardly, no matter how many times you have to repeat the same explanation. And on days when I've come to school, but my mind has been somewhere else, you've been quick to notice that I'm not myself and you've been sensitive to what's troubling me.

Thank you for your tireless efforts and for playing such an important role in my life. Your patient heart is an inspiration to me.

Sincerely,

Your Student

Patience and
fortitude conquer
all things.

RALPH WALDO EMERSON

Hold on; hold fast; hold out.

Patience is genius.

GEORGES-LOUIS LECLERC, COMTE DE BUFFON

GREAT TEACHERS

BY JEREMY MOORE

Great teachers are inspiring and bring out the best in us.

But the truly great teachers are the ones with patience.

I remember my high school math teacher, Mrs. Matlin. I had gone through eight years of public education absolutely hating math, and high school brought on the dreaded word: algebra.

X − 2 = 9. I know now that you solve for "X" and in this particular problem, X equals 11. I did not know that then, and to me it just looked like a scary piece of gibberish.

But Mrs. Matlin was a patient sort. Quiet and soft-spoken, she went over the same math problems again and again to a remedial algebra class that covered up their fear with insubordinate and obnoxious behavior.

Eventually she got through to us, and we learned algebra. I have not used algebra since, but I remember the satisfaction that I got from finally understanding.

Thank you, Mrs. Matlin.

I remember my writing teacher, Mr. Hanes.

By high school I had been told many times that I could write very well for someone my age, and I might have a future in writing as a career.

Praise like this has an odd effect on a high school freshman. We are already under the impression that we know everything, and compliments like that only make it worse.

But Mr. Hanes showed me I had a lot to learn. It was tough then, but I'm better for it now.

He said that I would one day make something of myself if I survived his class. I did, and I have. Thank you, Mr. Hanes, wherever you are.

I remember my gym teacher, Mr. Barnard.

Gym class is always tough for the fat kids. In grade school I was fat and uncoordinated, so gym was something I avoided as much as I could.

But Mr. Barnard looked out for kids like us, and he reminded the jocks who thought they were so great that their talents would not get them far if they did not lose their attitudes.

He told us fat, uncoordinated kids that it was just gym class, and we should have fun.

I did, for the first time.

Thank you, Mr. Barnard.

Truly great teachers are patient and understanding. They inspire us to become the very best that we can be.[4]

The strongest of all warriors

are these two—

Time and Patience.

Leo Tolstoy

Be of good cheer. Do not think of today's failures, but of the success that may come tomorrow. You have set yourselves a difficult task, but you will succeed if you persevere; and you will find a joy in overcoming obstacles. Remember, no effort that we make to attain something beautiful is ever lost.

HELEN KELLER

The end of a matter is better than its beginning,
and patience is better than pride.

ECCLESIASTES 7:8

🍎   🍎   🍎   🍎   🍎

Lord,

You are always so patient with me, even when I continue to make the same mistakes time and again. Sometimes I wonder how You do it.

My students keep a close tab on my level of patience. Some days it seems as if they're testing my patience more than I'm testing their knowledge of language or arithmetic!

Whenever I tell people I'm a teacher, a common response I get is, "I just wouldn't have the patience." Sometimes hearing this repeatedly tempts me to give in to my own weakness and to cut myself some slack in this area. However, that never works out very well, and I usually end up hurting my students and the relationships I've worked so hard to build with them.

It's then that I'm reminded of the higher standard I strive to hold myself to. You never lose your patience with me, and You are the example I wish to follow.

Help me to continually remember Your patience toward me so that I can pass that patience and grace along to my students. When they're having a rough day, help me to understand why they may be struggling rather than reacting from my own frustration.

Thank You for Your flawless example.

Amen.

I THANK GOD for you,

        my PATIENT teacher!

You're the

BEST

TEACHER

in the World Because...

You Care

About Me.

A child cannot be taught by anyone who despises him, and a child cannot afford to be fooled.

JAMES BALDWIN

Cast all your anxiety on him because he cares for you.

1 PETER 5:7

You genuinely care about each one of your students—his or her hopes, dreams, worries, disappointments. You want them all to succeed, not only in their academics, but in life. Though each year you have a new class—or maybe even multiple classes—of students, there is not one, either past or present, whom you don't hold dear and wish the best for. You want to see them all happy and fulfilled.

If you care that much about your students, think for a moment about how much your Heavenly Father must care for you. Sometimes we fool ourselves into believing that our small concerns are too trivial to take to God. After all, He has a whole world to look after. Why should He care that one person is having a bad day?

Yet He does care—very much in fact. And just as you feel honored when a student chooses to confide in you, God is delighted when you choose to trust Him with your concerns.

A LETTER TO MY TEACHER

Dear Teacher,

It's such a great feeling to know that my teacher genuinely cares about me and wants to see me succeed. I can't imagine how you do it—how you make each one of your many students feel that they are the most important person in the room—but somehow you do. And you don't seem to care simply about our grades. Sure, you want to see us do well and learn new ideas in your class, but you also show that you care about other areas of our lives. I've seen you at just about every ball game, cheering your students on. You're at all the plays and musicals too. You often ask about our families and brothers or sisters who were your previous students. I'm not sure how you find the time to do it all.

Thank you for your tireless efforts and your caring heart. I hope you're able to see the fruit of your labor and that your time will be multiplied as you give it away freely.

Sincerely,

Your Student

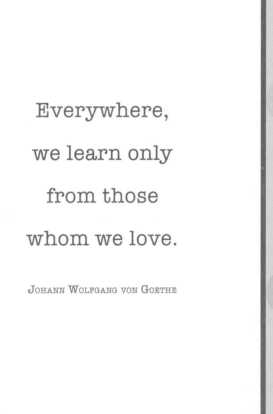

Everywhere,

we learn only

from those

whom we love.

<small>Johann Wolfgang von Goethe</small>

One looks back with appreciation to the
brilliant teachers, but with gratitude
to those who touched our human feelings.

CARL JUNG

A CARING TEACHER IS NEVER FORGOTTEN

By Renie Burghardt

When I began school in my new country, the United States of America, I was classified as a "Displaced Person." At age fourteen, *displaced* also described my fragile self-esteem. Horrors of the past had taken their toll on me. My family and I had lived through World War II in Hungary, followed by four years in a refugee camp, and *displaced* is exactly what we were.

So there I was—a mousy, shy D.P. girl—who spoke with a thick accent and was barely acknowledged by my beautiful American peers. For beautiful is what they were to me, those girls with their ponytails and carefree giggling ways, and I longed to be just like them. But I was different; my past still haunted me.

I attended an all-girls' Catholic school run by nuns, and the girls at that school came from all parts of the city we lived in, the older girls driving their own cars to get there. Of course, my family and I lived in a small rental house near the school, so we walked; and every time I entered the school, I did so with great trepidation, painfully aware of being different. I knew that it was a great sacrifice for my grandparents, who raised me, to send me there. We were newcomers to America, money was scarce in our household, and the school had tuition, uniform, and book expenses. But I felt lucky to have been accepted, since my English was still not quite up to par.

By the time June rolled around, I had been in my school six months. I was still shy, mousy, and barely noticed by the other girls, but despite the struggles to make my grades, I passed to the tenth grade. That was a relief! I spent that summer working part-time at a local dime store and hanging out with my friends at the shores of Lake Erie.

In September of that year, it was time to don the old blue-and-gold jumper and white blouse again and go back to school. I entered the building with the same trepidation and dread, and although some of the girls greeted me cheerily, I had not turned into a swan over the summer. But then I walked into Sister Eleanor's sophomore English class, and soon everything changed for the better.

Sister Eleanor had the bluest eyes, a smile that lit up the classroom, and a gentle, sympathetic, understanding manner. She seemed to instantly recognize my pain and, in front of the class, she began asking me questions about my life. She wanted my classmates to better understand why I was different from them. She explained the circumstances and gently encouraged them to put themselves in my shoes and see how they would feel in them. My mind quickly concluded that God had blessed me with one of His angels for a teacher. Then the good sister gave us all our first assignment of the new school term.

"I want you all to write an essay of at least four pages about something memorable that has recently happened to you. It will be due a week from today." When we left the classroom, I wasn't too sure what an essay was, but I put my heart and soul into that assignment.

I wrote about being crammed with hundreds of other immigrants on a ship taking us to our new country. I wrote about Dave, the young American who worked on that ship, befriended me, and bought me my first-ever Coke. I wrote about my first sight of the Statue of Liberty, and what a thrill that was, and about being processed at Ellis Island. I wrote about how it felt to be in a new country, where the language and customs were different. And as I wrote, I realized that I loved writing!

The day after we handed in our essays, Sister Eleanor had me read my essay aloud to the entire class. To my great surprise, my classmates applauded when I finished. Then I was sent to read it throughout the school and got the same reaction. Suddenly, girls mobbed me in the hallway, telling me how much they liked my essay, suggesting that I was a good writer, asking me questions, paying attention to me.

Suddenly, I was more than just a mousy D.P. girl—I was finally becoming a part of the group.

So two years later, when I tossed my cap in the air with my graduating class, I thought about Sister Eleanor. Because of her caring, understanding ways, the culture shock had been broken, and I was graduating as the confident, young American girl I longed to be. And to that gentle soul in the blue-and-white habit, I will always be grateful.[5]

The truth is that I

am enslaved . . .

in one vast love affair

with seventy children.

My high school English teacher not only encouraged me to become a writer, she cared about me as a person, too. She reviewed things that I had written outside of class and gave me great feedback. And when my family went through some difficult situations, she took the time to counsel me and pray with me. I knew that what happened to me mattered to her, and I will never forget how much she cared.

CHARLOTTE MAE

We lov'd the doctrine for the teacher's sake.

DANIEL DEFOE

Heavenly Father,

Thank You for caring about every minute detail of my life. You even know when a single hair falls from my head. Thank You that You care that much about each of my students too.

Some of my students are facing so many problems in their young lives that can seem overwhelming at times. Some of them go home to parents who are constantly fighting. Others are left to fend for themselves much of the time, with very little involvement from their families. Many have friends or siblings who struggle with drug or alcohol addictions, or maybe they even wrestle with these problems themselves. The list goes on and on.

Lord, their tender hearts need Your love and healing. Help me to be a source of comfort for them. Make my classroom a place of refuge from the storms that surround their lives. May it be an environment where they can lay down their cares and clear their minds to learn so they can make a better future for themselves than their present reality.

Please wrap each of my students in Your arms of love today.

Amen.

I THANK GOD for you,

my CARING teacher!

You're the

BEST

TEACHER

in the World Because…

You Take the

Time to Listen.

A teacher who takes the time

to listen will produce

students who are willing to learn.

F. NEWTON

Love the LORD your God, listen to his voice, and
hold fast to him. For the LORD is your life.

DEUTERONOMY 30:20

One of the ways you express your love to your students is by lending a listening ear whenever they have a question or need someone to talk to. Your willingness to listen to what they have to say and hear them out completely before interjecting your own ideas can be a catalyst for change in your students' lives, instilling confidence in them, a feeling of being important in the eyes of another.

A listening ear can be an expression of love to your Heavenly Father as well. When you take the time to be still and listen for His voice and His leading in your life, you're telling Him how much you respect His authority and cherish what He has to tell you. You're demonstrating His importance in your life.

As you say your prayers today, make sure you take time to listen as well.

A LETTER TO MY TEACHER

Dear Teacher,

I've never before had a teacher who was so willing to listen to what I have to say. When I ask you a question, you don't interrupt me with your answer, assuming that you already know what I'm asking. Instead, you listen intently to me until I'm finished. And when something we're talking about in class sparks an idea in me, you want to hear all about it. If there's no time in class, you're sure to make time afterward. When something is bothering me, you always seem to sense it, and you're quick to let me know that you're available if I want to talk about it.

Thank you for being such a good listener. You make me feel valued and important, that my ideas are well worth your time. I want you to know what a difference you've made in my life.

Sincerely,

Your Student

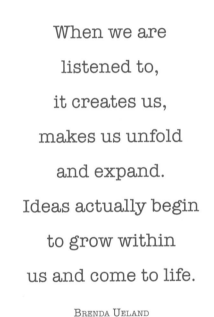

When we are

listened to,

it creates us,

makes us unfold

and expand.

Ideas actually begin

to grow within

us and come to life.

BRENDA UELAND

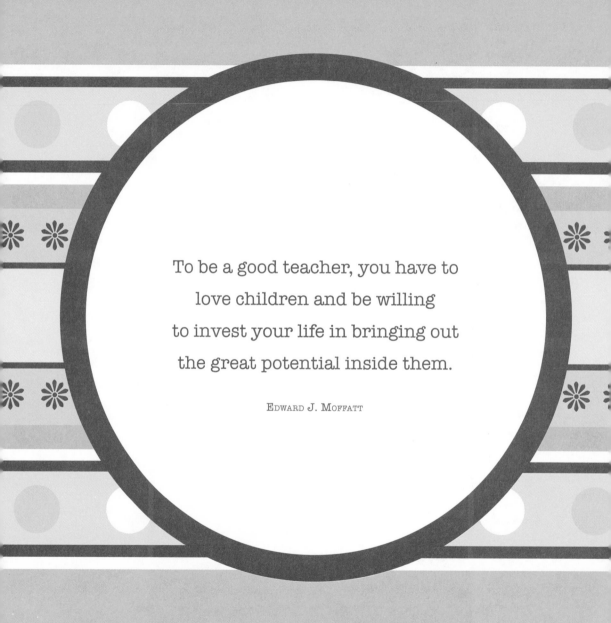

To be a good teacher, you have to
love children and be willing
to invest your life in bringing out
the great potential inside them.

MRS. BOYNTON

By Jeanne MacKenzie

The first day I walked into my fifth-grade classroom, I immediately surmised two crucial and intimate details about my new teacher, Mrs. Boynton. She wore a wig, and she was very old.

I'd recently turned ten, and my mind harbored a great deal of suspicion toward educators. Over the past five years, having easily learned the rudimentary basics they'd imparted, I had discovered at the same time it was kids like me who gave teachers an assortment of maladies including headaches, stomachaches, bald spots, and warts. Entering Mrs. Boynton's classroom, I was primed for another difficult year of school.

Instantly, my new teacher made it clear that she respected me. She told me I was smart, too, even in math. She really liked art and music, and as it turned out, so did I. It didn't take long before other kids started claiming that I had become the teacher's pet, but I didn't mind. It felt so good to be liked and appreciated by this woman. By that time, I had forgotten all about her wig, although she wore it every single day.

Mrs. Boynton made me realize that I was a valuable person, despite my youth and inexperience. My mother had been parenting me by herself. Her job made her tired; her boyfriends made her upset. She told me I demanded too much of her, and I started raising myself. Miraculously, Mrs. Boynton seemed to know this, even though I never told her.

"I'm here," she said, "if you ever want to talk to a grown-up who listens and cares about you." Her compassion brought tears to my eyes and, although I never did speak to her about home, it was enough to know that I could.

We read poetry every morning and learned to appreciate idealism and creativity. Mrs. Boynton presented a new poem every week, encouraging us to memorize all of them. I discovered it was easy to remember words and phrases that rhymed and flowed and made images in my mind. Today, when I write my own poetry, I often think of those times in the fifth grade, when all of us kids recited the poem of the week for Mrs. Boynton and, ultimately, for ourselves.

Above all, Mrs. Boynton taught me the importance of kindness toward others and the value of tact. One winter day, she rescued a tearful girl some boys had been teasing. She took her into the hallway and sat rocking her, swaying gently, and murmuring in her ear. Later on, during the spring, I ran in early from recess to tell Mrs. Boynton something. I stopped short in the doorway when I saw her holding up a dress to another girl in class. They both turned quickly when they heard me and I ran off before they could say anything. A few days later, the girl wore that dress to school and Mrs. Boynton acted like nothing had happened between them. Everybody knew that the girl was poor, including Mrs. Boynton.

Now, as I step into my own classroom of students every day, I am blessed with the opportunity to demonstrate those virtues of daily living. I will be forever thankful to Mrs. Boynton for sharing those beautiful pieces of herself with me.[6]

The best way to communicate your compassion is to listen with open ears and a caring heart.

D. Valentine

🍎 🍎 🍎 🍎 🍎

Heavenly Father,

Thank You for always having time for me. You're willing to listen to anything I bring to You—my concerns, my victories, even at times my whining and complaining. Not only are You willing to listen, but You take joy in each moment we spend together.

Make me sensitive to the times when one of my students needs a listening ear. Help me to slow down enough from my busy schedule to really hear what they're saying, and also what they may be too afraid to say. Give me the wisdom to know when to offer advice or instruction and when to be just a sounding board, someone they can depend on to simply understand.

I love each one of my students, and I want to communicate that to them through my willingness to hear them out. Open my ears, Lord, and also my heart.

Amen.

I THANK GOD for you,

my LISTENING teacher!

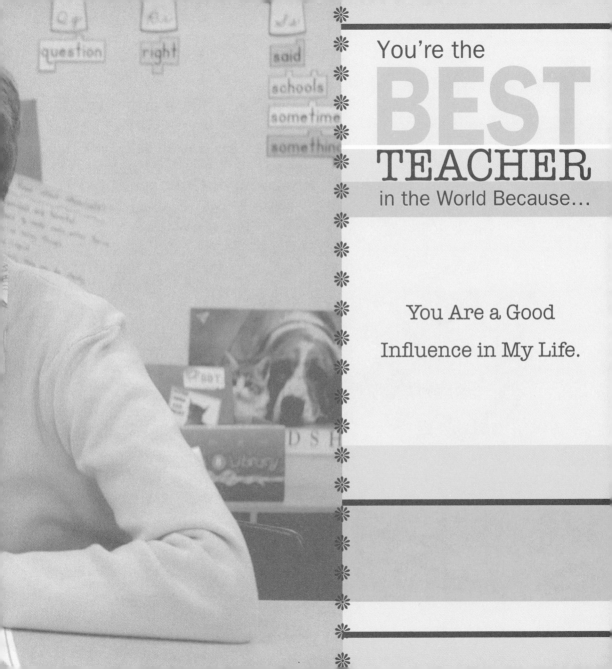

You're the

BEST
TEACHER
in the World Because…

You Are a Good
Influence in My Life.

A teacher affects eternity;

he can never tell

where his influence stops.

HENRY B. ADAMS

Jesus replied: "'Love the Lord your God with all your heart and with all your soul and with all your mind.' This is the first and greatest commandment. And the second is like it: 'Love your neighbor as yourself.' All the Law and the Prophets hang on these two commandments."

MATTHEW 22:37–40

Jesus, arguably the greatest teacher of all time, had tremendous influence over the people who listened to His instruction—much more than the religious teachers and scribes who prided themselves in their knowledge of the Bible. What was different about Jesus and His methods of teaching?

His entire philosophy was based on two very simple rules—love God and love other people. And He not only taught these important principles; He demonstrated them in his own life as well.

All the rules and theories and lists of knowledge in the world will not produce a change in the lives of your students as effectively as your simple example of a life lived out in love.

A LETTER TO MY TEACHER

Dear Teacher,

One thing I've never doubted since the moment I walked into your classroom that first day is that you genuinely love and care about each one of your students. You set high standards and expect us to live up to them, but you set even higher standards for yourself. And you live up to those standards in front of us, day after day. If you make a mistake, you are quick to correct yourself and offer an apology if one is in order. I've never known a person I would so like to emulate.

Thank you for your ceaseless efforts to live a pure life before your students. May your influence reach beyond your classroom into the lives of those with whom we, your students, come into contact.

Sincerely,

Your Student

Teaching is the greatest profession —
it allows you to mold
minds and hearts.

AUTHOR UNKNOWN

Praise is a great gift to give someone.
Praise is to the heart what water
is to a flower . . . life-giving.

R. Norton

LESSONS FROM MRS. FRANCIS

By Alison Simpson

When I was in the fifth grade, I had the privilege of being in Mrs. Francis's class. My older brother raved about her when he heard she would be my teacher. He, along with the rest of the school, loved her . . . thought she was the best teacher ever. She was fun, she was smart, and she was always one step ahead of her students. No one could get anything past her, but everyone still loved her and thought she was the coolest teacher in the school.

The memory of Mrs. Francis that I cherish the most (other than our class making Christmas cookies at her house one Saturday morning) was when I was struggling with long division. I hated long division, and I was *awful* at it. I'm not exaggerating about this—math in general was way over my head. And, sure enough, my homework assignments revealed to Mrs. Francis that I was most definitely in need of help.

One afternoon after class, Mrs. Francis told me she was putting a note to my parents in my backpack. At first I was horrified. But then she explained that she wanted to help me, and she wanted permission to keep me after class. I reluctantly presented the note to my mom, and she agreed that from now on, I'd spend two days a week after school, trying to master long division with Mrs. Francis.

And my fears were correct . . . it was frustrating and hard. I remember sitting in the front row of desks staring at the blackboard while she showed me how to work problems, and I felt clueless. Then she had me up at the blackboard, asking me to try, affirming my answers when they were right, and tenderly correcting them when they were wrong. Somehow, faced with a challenge I felt for sure I'd never master, she made me feel like I was smart. She helped me see that I could get this, with perseverance, patience, and a positive attitude.

Not only did she teach me long division, but she also taught me that it was worth it to her to help me. *Why?* I wondered. She could have sent a note home to my parents saying, "Alison is not grasping long division. Please work with her on this." But she didn't pass the buck. She decided that this was a perfect opportunity to help me see what I could do, and she knew she could help make it happen for me. She took me on as her responsibility because she cared enough about me not only as a student but also as a person.

Challenges are not opportunities for failure . . . they're invitations to grow. I learned that best when I was standing at the blackboard with Mrs. Francis. As hard as long division seemed to me, she taught me that it's possible for me to face my fear and then move on to bigger and better challenges. It's all part of being the best kind of me that I can be. Smaller challenges lead to bigger challenges, but the concept is the same: Patience, a positive attitude, and perseverance are three "must-haves" in your toolbox for life. If you've got those things ready and available to you, you can tackle just about anything that comes your way in life.[7]

The depth of your influence depends upon
the power of your example.

PABLO DEL POZO

Lord,

I want my students to learn the material I'm teaching them, but more than anything, my hope is that I'll be a positive influence on their character. I want them to be able to look back on their time in my classroom with fond memories and maybe take away something that will help them to be better citizens or parents or leaders in the future.

Influencing young minds and hearts can be a rather daunting responsibility at times, and I need Your constant help. Please guide my words and actions as I strive to be the example these students need.

Thank You for trusting me with this responsibility. Help me to never take it for granted or become careless with my behavior around my students. I count it a great privilege to be placed in such a position of influence. You're so good to me.

Amen.

I THANK GOD for you,

my INFLUENCING teacher!

You're the

BEST

TEACHER

in the World Because...

You Bring Out the

Best in Me.

No one has yet
fully realized the
wealth of sympathy,
kindness, and
generosity hidden in
the soul of a child.
The effort of
every true education
should be to unlock
that treasure.

EMMA GOLDMAN

God has given each of us the ability to do certain things well.

ROMANS 12:6 NLT

God has equipped you with the personality and a unique set of skills that make you ideal for teaching. In the same way, He is equipping each of your students. What a privilege you've been given to play an important role in that process.

As you detect certain abilities in your students, see if you can find creative ways to allow them to put those abilities to use. Perhaps one of your students has administrative abilities and would enjoy helping you grade or record papers. Another might be a good encourager and be able to help students who are falling behind. Someone in your class may have an artistic flair and be able to assist you with bulletin boards. Sharing these responsibilities with your students when possible will build their confidence and may help them to discover their own unique talents.

During your prayer time, remember to pray that each of your students will develop the skills that are unique to them and will discover God's path for them.

A LETTER TO MY TEACHER

Dear Teacher,

I know for certain that you believe in me. You let me know in so many ways—by asking me about my progress in my areas of interest, by giving me responsibilities that you could certainly handle better yourself, and by praising me when I participate in class. And your belief in me rubs off; when I'm around you, I feel as if I could accomplish anything I set my mind to.

Thank you for seeing value in me and for working so hard to bring out my potential. You've made such a difference in the way I see myself. I want to make you proud.

Sincerely,

Your Student

Dear God,

Help me to be a nurturer—to love my students and invest my life in them. Help me to bring out the treasure that You have put inside each one of them. Thank You for the privilege of teaching them.

R. Norton

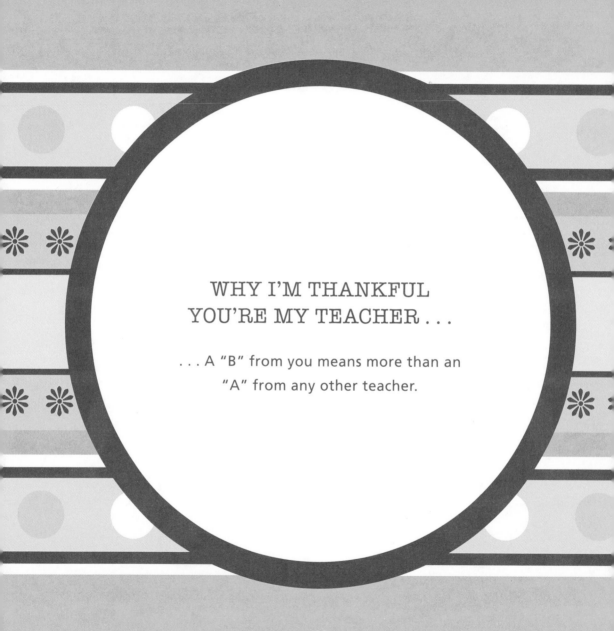

WHY I'M THANKFUL
YOU'RE MY TEACHER...

...A "B" from you means more than an
"A" from any other teacher.

A TRIBUTE TO MANY UNCROWNED KINGS AND QUEENS

Dr. Daniel Eckstein

In the spring of 1962, I was in the seventh grade at Johnnycake Junior High School in Baltimore—Section 7B to be precise. In earlier years, the distinctions between classes had been the "redbirds" and the "bluebirds" in a vain attempt to avoid labeling one class the smart one and the other class (mine) the "dummy" group. But we all knew who was who in the hierarchy of redbirds and bluebirds. So in seventh grade the pretense was dropped in favor of 7A and 7B.

All my neighborhood friends were in the coveted A class. Me? I majored in playground. I was an "honor" student—as in, "Yes, Your Honor. No, Your Honor. I won't do that anymore, Your Honor."

I was a classic left-handed, dyslexic, hyperactive boy who consistently received "unsatisfactory" conduct scores under the category vaguely defined as "self-control." The letters M and N were indistinguishable to me, and a D masqueraded as B, P, or Q. Classes were much too long, the desks far too small, and the outdoor activities way too short. Like a prisoner about to be granted a three-month furlough, I was counting down the days until June.

The teacher for both 7A and 7B was like a great redwood tree to me; a colossal giant who at six feet, two inches tall seemed twice as awesome from my diminished vantage point. Mr. King was his well-named title. He was kind, knowledgeable, and revered by both sections A and B, a rare feat for any teacher.

One day, quite unexpectedly, Mr. King approached my 7A friends and observed that, "There is someone in 7B who is just as smart as any of you. Trouble is, he just doesn't know it yet. I won't tell you his name, but I'll give you a hint—he's the kid who outruns all of you and knocks the ball over the right-field fence."

Word of Mr. King's declaration reached me that afternoon as we boarded the school bus. I remember a dazed, shocked feeling of disbelief. "Yeah, sure. You've got to be kidding," I nonchalantly replied to my friends; but on a deeper, more subtle level, I remember the warm glow that came from the tiny flicker of a candle that had been ignited within my soul.

Two weeks later, it was time for the dreaded book reports in front of the class. It was bad enough to turn in papers that only Mr. King read, but there was no place to hide when it came to oral book reports.

When my turn came, I solemnly stood before my classmates. I began slowly and awkwardly to speak about James Fenimore Cooper's epic book *The Pathfinder.* As I spoke, the images of canoes on the western frontier of eighteenth-century America collided with lush descriptions of the forest and Native Americans who glided noiselessly over lakes and streams. No Fourth of July fireworks have ever surpassed the explosion that took place inside my head that day—it was electrifying! Excitedly, I began trying to share them all with my classmates. But just as I began a sentence to tell about the canoes, another scene of the land collided with one of Native Americans. I was only midway through one sentence before I jumped to another. I was "hyper" in my joy, and my incomplete sentences made no sense at all.

The laughter of my classmates at my "craziness" quickly shattered my inner fireworks. Embarrassed and humiliated, I wanted to either beat up my tormentors or to run home and cry in my mother's arms. But I'd learned how to mask those feelings long ago. So I returned to my desk, trying to become invisible.

The laughter ceased at the sound of Mr. King's deep, compassionate voice. "You know, Danny," he reigned forth, "you have a unique gift; the ability to speak outwardly and to think inwardly at the same time. But sometimes your mind is filled with so much joy that your words just can't keep up. Your excitement is contagious—it's a wonderful gift that I hope you can put to good use someday."

There was a pause that seemed to linger forever as I stood stunned, and then it began—clapping and congratulatory cheers from my classmates. A miracle of transformation occurred within me on that great day.

Forty years later, I now have fancy-sounding words like "encouragement" or "turning a perceived minus into a plus" to describe what Mr. King did for me that day. Today, I take my turn to say "thank you" to all the Mr. and Ms. Kings—the teachers who helped me and countless others reframe our lives forever.[8]

A teacher is one who instills

in others the knowledge,

motivation, and courage to

follow their destiny.

AUTHOR UNKNOWN

Mr. Shelton always made me want to do my best in his class. It was always harder than the others, but that's what made a good grade so worthwhile. Learning wasn't a drag in his class, though — he always managed to make it fun. I think that's what makes a teacher great — inspiring you to work hard but helping you to have a good time while you're doing it.

PHILLIP E. WAINWRIGHT

> Children should be led into the right paths,
> not by severity, but by persuasion.
>
> TERENCE, 186–159 B.C.E

Heavenly Father,

It's incredible to me that You can know everything about me—each selfish thought or dishonest action—yet still love me and believe in me. In fact, since I've accepted Your forgiveness through the sacrifice of Your Son, You see me as righteous, holy, even perfect. It's because of this great love that I desire to live up to Your view of me.

Father, help me to see past the weaknesses in my students so that I might tap into their true potential. Many of my students are discouraged and lack confidence because they don't exhibit qualities that are conducive to classroom-style learning. Some of them have trouble concentrating in class because they're too busy keeping up with the latest happenings around the school. If encouraged in the right direction, they could be great reporters someday. Others can be disruptive at times because of their comedic inclinations, but they could turn out to be valuable mediators with their ability to ease tension.

Help me to find the unique talent in each of my students and to encourage them to develop these strengths. When I need to correct a disruptive student, help me to do it in a manner that is constructive and encouraging. You have a special plan for each of my students. Give me creative ideas as I attempt to guide them toward that plan today.

Amen.

I THANK GOD for you,

my MOTIVATING teacher!

You're the

BEST

TEACHER

in the World Because…

You Inspire Me to

Achieve My Dreams.

The mediocre teacher tells.

The good teacher explains.

The superior teacher demonstrates.

The great teacher inspires.

WILLIAM ARTHUR WARD

Take delight in the Lord, and he will give you
your heart's desires. Commit everything you do to the Lord.
Trust him, and he will help you.

PSALM 37:4-5 NLT

Is there a dream you've envisioned for your classroom that just hasn't come to fruition despite all your efforts? If so, don't give up on it. Often those creative ideas that spring into your mind are nothing less than divine inspiration. A roadblock here or there doesn't necessarily mean that it just wasn't meant to be.

The best thing to do when you run into obstacles is to take your idea to God in prayer. Ask Him for confirmation about whether the idea was inspired by His Spirit. Consider your motives for wanting to see your dream come about. Are your motives unselfish and based on a desire to help others and to glorify God? Or are they based on a desire to gain the approval of your peers and administration?

If your motives are pure and the idea was from God, press on. At the right time, your dream will become a reality.

A LETTER TO MY TEACHER

Dear Teacher,

I've had people tell me to follow my dreams before, but never someone as willing as you are to dream right along with me. If you see something I'm good at, you let me know, and you're excited about telling me all the possibilities that skill could hold for my future. If I confide in you about something I enjoy or would like to try, you're right there, encouraging me and doing what you can to make it happen. No ambition is too great or unusual for you to believe your students can succeed at it, and you put everything you have into helping us achieve our dreams.

Thank you for being a dreamer and for believing the impossible. I want to live up to the faith you've placed in me.

Sincerely,

Your Student

Education is not

the filling of a pail,

but the

lighting of a fire.

WILLIAM BUTLER YEATS

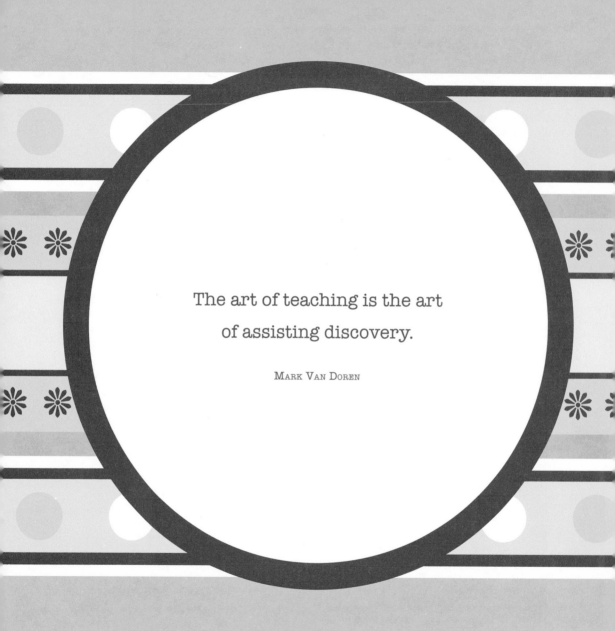

The art of teaching is the art
of assisting discovery.

MARK VAN DOREN

OLD CROW

BY MARY COOK

The Victorian school building stood out like a decaying tooth in the mouth of hell, surrounded as it was by the desolation of postwar Britain. But a dashing war hero was to lead me beyond the ruins.

Arundel Street Junior Mixed School was in the center of Portsmouth on the south coast of England. A major naval port, the city had lost about one-third of its homes and business premises to German bombs.

Alastair Crowley-Smith, my class teacher, was a man of many passions. And he had a talent to convey them to others. No dry academic, he lived and breathed whatever subject he was teaching at any one time. An ex-fighter pilot, he'd been shot down three times by enemy fire.

I was going to marry him when I grew up. The fact that he was already married with five children meant nothing to my eight-year-old mind. Coy about my crush on him, I referred privately to Mr. Crowley-Smith as "Old Crow."

Thoroughly steeped in the arts, he was an ardent admirer of Vincent van Gogh. He brought in a reproduction of the artist's *Sunflowers*. We painted sunflowers that looked like blobs of yellow paint.

But then he told us the story of how van Gogh had gone mad

and cut off part of his ear—stirring stuff for first-year juniors. We felt inspired to paint sunflowers with fresh vigor.

He collected fistfuls of bluebells, and we streaked our paper with the searing purple-blues that we found in our pastel tins.

Another of Mr. Crowley-Smith's passions was archaeology. He devised a house system in which we were divided into teams of Romans, Normans, Saxons, and Vikings. One day he came into class carrying a brown paper bag containing numerous fragments of Roman pottery. When he asked who would like a piece to keep, thirty-plus hands shot ceilingward.

He walked around the room, placing a potsherd on each child's desk. I handled my fragment reverently out of respect for the toga-clad individual whose long-dead fingers had created the pot and decorated it with cross-hatching.

That day we made Roman-style pots from modeling clay.

Mr. Crowley-Smith loved poetry and drama. A talented actor, he was a leading light in the Southsea Shakespeare Actors. He also introduced us to the traditional poetry of the Border Ballads. My favorite was Lord Randall, with its story of a young lord poisoned by his sweetheart. I particularly enjoyed intoning the chilling refrain: "Mother, make my bed soon, for I'm weary wi' hunting and fain would lie doon. . . ."

In those days, the way you spoke mattered. If you let it be known you came from a poor background, you stayed poor. But Mr. Crowley-Smith raised our sights by giving us the social advantages that came with elocution lessons.

Mr. Crowley-Smith taught us that figures were important in everyday life, but I never mastered those. When he called on me in class to answer a math question, I was a rabbit caught in the glare of his headlights. No, make that headlight—he rode a drop handlebar gold racing bike. We children fought among ourselves for the honor of wheeling it into school.

In the unlikely event of his still being alive, Mr. Crowley-Smith would be proud to know that somewhere there is a moderately successful writer who was one of his "mixed juniors." I'd like to thank him for his valuable lessons. And though I suspect he knew it went with the territory, I'd want to apologize for dogging his footsteps with my puppy-like devotion. But he truly inspired me to achieve my dreams.[9]

A teacher plants "dream" seeds

in her students and

waters them with loving care.

VICTORIA CRANK

WHY I'M THANKFUL
YOU'RE MY TEACHER . . .

. . . You believe that I can be anything
I want to be.

The ability to inspire students to dream about what they could become is a gift bestowed from heaven above.

VALENCIA SMITH

Lord,

You placed a dream in my heart many years ago to be an inspiration and a mentor to young people. Now You've made that dream a reality through my role as a teacher. Father, I'll admit that, at times, my job doesn't seem so much like a dream come true. In the midst of piles of paperwork and discipline problems, I sometimes lose sight of how blessed I am to be used by You to influence young minds in such a way.

Thank You for placing this dream in my heart and for making it come about. Even with all its challenges, I wouldn't trade teaching for the world. I love my students and take joy in the ability You've given me to inspire them to follow their dreams.

Some of my students have huge dreams. Help me to know how to provide the tools they need to make those dreams become a reality. I want to be a source of encouragement and confidence for them. For those of my students who don't yet have a dream for their futures, may they feel inspired in my classroom to think big, to begin imagining the vast possibilities before them. May they know, as I do, the wonderful fulfillment that comes from seeking after the dreams You instill in us.

Amen.

I THANK GOD for you,

my INSPIRING teacher!

If we work upon marble, it will perish; if we work upon brass, time will efface it; if we rear temples, they will crumble into dust. But if we work on immortal minds, if we imbue them with high principles, with the just fear of God and love of their fellowmen, we engrave on those tablets something which no time can efface, but which will brighten all eternity.

DANIEL WEBSTER

What nobler employment is there
than that of the person
who instructs the rising generation?

CICERO

* * * * *

If we succeed in giving the love of learning,
the learning itself is sure to follow.

JOHN LUBBOCK

NOTES

[1] Carrie Younce, Escondido, California. Story used by permission of the author.
[2] Robin Lee Shope, Flower Mound, Texas. Story used by permission of the author.
[3] Shae A. Cooke, Port Coquitlam, BC, Canada. Story used by permission of the author.
[4] Jeremy Moore, Turnersville, New Jersey. Story used by permission of the author.
[5] Renie Burghardt, Doniphan, Missouri. Story used by permission of the author.
[6] Jeanne MacKenzie, Rimrock, Arizona. Story used by permission of the author.
[7] Alison Simpson, Frankfort, Kentucky. Story used by permission of the author.
[8] Daniel Eckstein, Ph.D. Story used by permission of the author.
[9] Mary Cook, Alford, Lincolnshire, England. Story used by permission of the author.

LOOK FOR THESE BOOKS:

THE BEST FRIEND
IN THE WORLD

THE BEST GRANDMA
IN THE WORLD

THE BEST SISTER
IN THE WORLD

HOWARD BOOKS
A DIVISION OF SIMON & SCHUSTER
New York   London   Toronto   Sydney